Fragments of a Farewell Letter
Read by Geologists

Fragments of a Farewell Letter Read by Geologists

Normand Chaurette

translated by Linda Gaboriau

Talonbooks
1998

Published with the assistance of the Canada Council.

Talonbooks
#104—3100 Production Way
Burnaby, British Columbia, Canada V5A 4R4

Typeset in Garamond and printed and bound in Canada by Hignell Printing.

First Printing: November 1998

Talonbooks are distributed in Canada by General Distribution Services, 325 Humber College
Blvd., Toronto, Ontario, Canada M9W 7C3; Tel.:(416) 213-1919; Fax:(416) 213-1917.
Talonbooks are distributed in the U.S.A. by General Distribution Services Inc.,
85 Rock River Drive, Suite 202, Buffalo, New York, U.S.A. 14207-2170; Tel.:1-800-805-1083;
Fax:1-800-481-6207.

Fragments d'une lettre d'adieu lus par des géologues was first published in French in 1986
by Leméac Éditeur, Montréal, Québec.

Canadian Cataloguing in Publication Data

Chaurette, Normand, 1954-
  [Fragments d'une lettre d'adieu lus par des géologues. English]
  Fragments of a farewell letter read by geologists

  A play.
  Translation of: Fragments d'une lettre d'adieu lus par des géologues.
  ISBN 0-88922-400-5

  I. Title. II. Title: Fragments d'une lettre d'adieu lus par des géologues. English.
PS8555.H439F7213 1998 C842'.54   C98-910722-1
PQ3919.2.C5316F7213 1998

Fragments d'une lettre d'adieu lus par des géologues was first produced in French by Théâtre de Quat'Sous in Montreal, on March 8, 1988, with the following cast:

LLOYD MACURDY. . . . . . Larry-Michel Demers
JASON CASSILLY . . . . Jean-Guy Viau
RALPH PETERSON . . . . Pierre Drolet
DAVID LENOWSKI . . . . Martin Drainville
NIKOLS OSTWALD . . . . Jean-Louis Roux
CARLA VAN SAIKIN. . . . . Anne Caron
XU SOJEN . . . . Daniel Dô
Directed by Michel Forgues
Designed by Danièle Lévesque
Lighting by Lysanne Desmarais
Costumes by Suzanne Ferland

Fragments of a Farewell Letter Read by Geologists was first produced in English by Equity Showcase Theatre in Toronto, on October 21, 1992, with the following cast:

LLOYD MACURDY. . . . . . . Todd Sandomirsky
JASON CASSILLY . . . . Michael Albert
RALPH PETERSON . . . . Ric Waugh
DAVID LENOWSKI . . . . Michael Carley
NIKOLS OSTWALD. . . . . John Ralston
CARLA VAN SAIKIN . . . . Denise Norman
XU SOJEN . . . . Jovanni Sy
Directed by Ian Prinsloo
Sets and Costumes designed by Cheryl Mills
Lighting by Bonnie Beecher
Composer and Musician: Doug Innis
Consulting Director: D.D. Kugler
Movement Consultant: Paula Thomson

*For Michel, who, one rainy, bluesy evening,
asked me to write him a play about rivers.
Like a dictionary of waterways.
Thanks to him, there began,
with my pen in an enormous atlas,
an unforgettable trip around the world.*

*I would also like to thank engineer Michael C. Turcot
for his patience and his generosity.*

CHARACTERS AND SETTING

A round table. An inquiry into the failure of a scientific expedition in Cambodia. From left to right:

LLOYD MACURDY, age 28, geologist
JASON CASSILLY, age 30, geologist
RALPH PETERSON, age 34, geologist
DAVID LENOWSKI, age 27, geologist
NIKOLS OSTWALD, age 50, chairman of the inquiry
CARLA VAN SAIKIN, age 32, doctor
XU SOJEN, engineer. He is ageless.

On the table, glasses of water, pencils, papers, magnifying glasses. But most of all, reports. Many reports. Tons of reports. The geologists have all this within reach: documents, written things. Proof. They are going to read.

All the characters, including Carla van Saikin and Xu Sojen who will only speak at the end, remain on stage, seated, throughout the whole play. A septet: the performers follow their scores even when they are not playing. In fact, their silences are written into the play.

All three movements are performed in succession and without an intermission. Like the geologists' testimonies, both Carla van Saikin's and Xu Sojen's monologues are part of the inquiry which runs the length of the entire play.

I

The Blue Nile, The Mekong

LLOYD MACURDY

I included the fragments of Toni van Saikin's farewell letter as an appendix to my report on the expedition. I don't know how important you will find them. For all intents and purposes, we are talking about several barely legible pages. He had them on him at the time of his death. Water erased most of the passages. We don't know what he did with the rest.

Nor do we know over how long a period Toni van Saikin wrote this letter. It was July when we first noticed that he was writing assiduously, every evening, sometimes late into the night. We thought he was recording his observations on the progress of our operations. He never showed us what he was writing. And he wasn't very talkative. We had no way of knowing exactly what was on his mind. He had not confided to anyone that he was going to die.

The first fragment reads as follows: *When you read these lines, in this god-forsaken part of the world ...*

The second fragment: *When you read these lines, on this shore beyond all landmarks ... on the banks of this river ...*

One can barely decipher the third fragment: *By the time you have read these lines ...*

The rest is more or less illegible.

Mr. Chairman ...

Mr. Chairman, it was just over a year ago that we got the idea of organizing an expedition in tropical territory in order to test a system of water purification and transformation, using a unit invented by engineer Toni van Saikin. We received most of our funding from the American government. The Minnesota Geological Research Center supplied the necessary equipment, the instruments, the cameras, the enlarged scale models, the missing components of the meccano structure. St. Paul University authorized the expedition after our paper had been read and approved.

The date of departure had been set for April 15th. The rainy season was beginning over there. A young apprentice had joined our ranks to study atmospheric conditions. According to Toni van Saikin who had conceived the entire project, it was essential that the unit be tested when the water level reached its highest point; at a certain time of the year, depending upon the floods, this water level makes it possible to achieve a geothermal capacity up to one hundred times greater than its hydroelectric potential. Our stilling tank contained gases, steam or water, as well as pressurized methane, in order to keep the rocks dry, the latter having been cooled off by a fluid derived from an external source. The primary obstacle arose from the fact that we could not count on solar energy to produce synthesizing fuel. To compensate for this, a system of artificial distribution of hydraulic energy had been included as part of the evaporation cycle of the water reserves. This way, we could use the energy directly, either for heating the camp or for producing electricity.

As soon as we arrived in Khartoum, we noticed a malfunction in the main turbine. Closer inspection showed that one of the cylinders was tilted too far in relation to the spiral's axis. There were two possible solutions: l. sacrifice the spare turbine and operate the sorting spinner by hand; 2. tilt the spiral's axis until it was parallel with the defective cylinder. In both cases, we were running the risk of seriously damaging the unit. Finally Toni van Saikin opted for replacing the defective cylinder and filling the sorter by hand … We were going to have to spell each other, day and night, for six months, Mr. Chairman.

Towards the end of April, the water reserves coming from the feeding channel showed that the sediments collected in the riverbed of the Blue Nile could not be dissolved using carbonic gas. We would have had to dig down three hundred feet to find organic debris with reduced deposits, an operation our modest equipment did not allow us to undertake. That is when Toni van Saikin decided to change the itinerary and the dates we'd agreed upon and travel on to Cambodia in early May. The subterranean waters of the Mekong, especially at the mouth of the river, at Prak-Kèk, offered a saturated superficial layer with a greatly reduced level of oxygen, because of the low amount of sulphur dioxide in this region of the Asia.

NIKOLS OSTWALD

You … You did say: sulphur dioxide?

LLOYD MACURDY

Yes, Mr. Chairman. Sulphur dioxide.

NIKOLS OSTWALD

That's strange ... In approximately what proportion?

LLOYD MACURDY

Good heavens ... I must have it written down
somewhere ...

NIKOLS OSTWALD

It doesn't matter, go on ...

LLOYD MACURDY

Something like zero point eight per cent.

NIKOLS OSTWALD

Go on.

LLOYD MACURDY

From July on, it's very difficult for us to place the
events in chronological order. So with your
permission, Mr. Chairman, I would simply like to
enumerate the causes which in my opinion explain
the failure of this expedition.

It goes without saying that the malfunction of the
unit is the principal reason. Also, the fact that we
hadn't foreseen the magnitude of the rains and the
floods in Cambodia. Our base camp consisted of a
meccano structure that we had to set up on a muddy
terrain, a terrain that threatened to shift at any
moment. None of the risks had been calculated. To
this day we have trouble understanding why Toni van
Saikin changed the itinerary of our expedition so
abruptly.

Mr. Chairman, I have nothing to reveal to you. Nor
do I have anything to hide from you. Like everyone

else, I expressed my objections, but we were the ones who had appointed Toni van Saikin to lead the expedition. Given the circumstances beyond our control, and given the fact that there were so few of us, it seemed judicious to trust the man who had conceived the project and who, in the final analysis, was the only one who believed in it. He believed in it with such determination that not one of us was capable of convincing him there was any reason to drop the experiment. We were dealing with a stubborn man. We were also dealing with a man who had decided to die, I am personally convinced of that. It has been said repeatedly that this expedition failed because engineer Toni van Saikin died. I think, on the contrary, that Toni van Saikin died because the expedition was bound to fail no matter what. He knew it as well as the rest of us. I think he couldn't bear the thought. But all of this remains a hypothesis.

Mr. Chairman, Gentlemen, Madam, I thank you for your attention.

JASON CASSILLY

Mr. Chairman, Gentlemen, Madam ...

You will find Toni van Saikin's farewell letters in the appendix to this report. There are eight pages in all. Two are perfectly legible:

When you read these lines, in this god-forsaken part of the world ...

When you read these lines, on this shore far from all landmarks ...

One is more difficult to decipher:

By the time you have read these lines ...

... and five where humidity has completely erased the ink, which was an oil-based preparation containing pigments probably derived from cephalopoda that simply disintegrated when exposed to a reagent composed of a specific chloride and hydrogen, in this case the water from the tropical rains.

Toni van Saikin started writing as soon as he arrived in Cambodia. We didn't know that what he was writing was a farewell letter. We didn't know he intended to die. This is, however, the conclusion we reached when we realized that he never wrote anything remotely resembling scientific notes or reports. Not even a diary. Only these rough drafts.

Mr. Chairman, since we have to vacate this hearing room by ten o'clock, I shall read only the essential points of my report to this inquiry. As far as the origins of the project are concerned, I would simply like to remind you that the study submitted to the National Research Center a year ago was on the gradual transformation and erosion effects of river waters. In order to prevent the erosion of the banks of the Mississippi in the state of Wisconsin, engineer Toni van Saikin had already devised an installation designed to retain the waters in a specific reach and to transform the wastes contained in those reserves into decomposable material in order to facilitate biodegradation. There is one such plant in Cape Girardeau and another downstream in Newport, Arkansas. Toni van Saikin had these installations in mind when he built his unit designed to accomplish both the extraction of underwater sediments and water purification in tropical regions.

The goal of this expedition was of an essentially humanist nature. *(Pause, he corrects himself.)* An essentially humanitarian nature, I mean. Aware, as we were, of the problems of malnutrition and drought in developing regions, we set ourselves the goal of exploring the sediments extracted from the riverbeds of the territorial waters of Africa and Southeast Asia, of purifying these waters by filtering the residues and classifying or separating the denser molecules obtained by using a spiral turbine operated on hydraulic pressure, in order to treat the recuperated water while retaining it in a chamber equipped with bidirectional valves attached to two delivery meters capable of alternating their energy forces: a single-cylinder turbine upstream and a final-phase purifier operating with the help of a magnetic field downstream. The idea per se was childishly simple. It did, however, require testing.

Mr. Chairman, I feel it is safe to say at this point in the inquiry that our colleague, Toni van Saikin, was an idealist. A great engineer, true, an inventor, a person of phenomenal intelligence, but first and foremost an idealist. His faith moved mountains, but if you'll forgive my saying so, it was not able to put an end to the rains. Throughout all six months of the expedition, from April through October, it rained. The flooding of the Mekong brought about a shifting and sliding of the terrain the likes of which had never before been seen in that region. We had to interrupt our operations several times a day. As early as July, we knew that this expedition would be a failure. But Toni van Saikin kept telling us to wait. Other than that, he said very little else. He wrote.

As far as the rest of my report is concerned, I think it reconfirms much of what has been said so far. It relates a series of accidents and circumstances, unfortunate conditions and unlucky events which upset our plans. Our defective radio set. The meccano structure erected on muddy ground, the rains, the floods, the presence of species with cheliceral appendages, arachnids like scorpions and water-scorpions, a veritable colony of carnivorous insects, iguanas, snakes and other protero-reptilian species, the breakdown of communications between Phnom-Penh and Minneapolis, the malfunction in the single-cylinder turbine, the lack of provisions, the lack of drinking water, and finally the death of engineer Toni van Saikin.

Before turning the floor over to my colleague, Ralph Peterson, I would like to share with the members of this inquiry my recommendations concerning the need to ensure in the future greater control and particularly a better communications system. It seems totally unacceptable to me that more than ten days went by between the day we reported Toni van Saikin's death and the day engineer Xu Sojen was sent to the site. If an expedition similar to this one were to take place again, emergency measures should be provided for, in the event of shortages, mechanical breakdowns, bad weather and any other imponderables which, in our case, went as far as the loss of a human life. I would like to thank you for your attention.

RALPH PETERSON

I would like to thank my friend and colleague Jason Cassilly for his recommendations which I endorse, and which add to the ... if I may use the word ... *humanist* aspect of his presentation.

Mr. Chairman, Gentlemen, Madam, on the last page of my report, you will find a copy of the fragments of Toni van Saikin's farewell letter. Five of them are illegible. But it is possible to get an idea of what one might have read in those pages, recovered from their sojourn in the river, based on the fact that the legible fragments—of which there are three for a total of eight—say with more or less the same words, more or less the same things.

When you read these lines ...
When you read these lines ...
By the time you have read these lines ...

Mr. Chairman, just over a year ago, we received authorization from the National Research Center to travel to tropical territory, more precisely, to the Sudan and to Cambodia, where we were to test the sediments extracted from the riverbeds and, subsequently, using a chamber equipped with bidirectional valves, reduce the level of toxic residue in order to purify the irrigation water. As we all know, Toni van Saikin was appointed to lead the expedition.

Our departure was a joyous occasion. Although we had intended to leave in March, we were forced to wait until April 15th, because of the delays caused by a never-ending series of procedures. Getting permission to enter the Sudan is no easy matter, and Cambodia is even harder. Toni van Saikin knew it, but he didn't seem remotely worried by the cautionary tales from External Affairs and from some Swiss friends who had lived there. On the contrary, the idea that Air America pilots often get lost in the mists and their aircraft crash into the mountains of the Xieng Khouang appealed to that engineer who loved taking risks and thrived on danger. I was in charge of our visas and the list of my comings and goings to various embassies and passport offices, to State Departments, mission headquarters, border stations, Triclinium, harems, huts and abodes, as well as to all the places administered by our troops, would be as long as the list of all my purchases, stamps, photocopies, shipping bills and customs fees, sometimes higher than the cost of the presents. Despite the bribes, our visas for Cambodia were refused three times in a row by the Deputy Minister of External Affairs. We had to wait several days and listen to hours of trivial chatter, before we finally managed to get into the Thai Embassy, since we had to travel through Thailand, where everything American has been outlawed, except the dollar. They suspected us of wanting to go into the villages to spread another ideology. The fact that we couldn't speak a single Asian dialect didn't seem to convince the ADCDLJ office of the legitimacy of our expedition. Those people had no more interest in geology than we had in their noodle soup. The World Bank had to intervene again and we finally were granted a short-term visa for Phnom-Penh, with permission to travel into the jungle as long as we were accompanied by Good Will workers, volunteers from a humanitarian organization.

The atmosphere when we finally left Minnesota on April 15th was one of enthusiasm on the way to New York, euphoria on the way to London, exhaustion on the way to Athens and perplexity upon arrival Khartoum. Our mood was becoming gloomy as they say in the weather forecasts, and by the time we reached the Sudan, driving rain had begun and we learned from Stanley La Paz that April showers bring May flowers is not a tropical saying.

Two tests took place in Khartoum, both rather inconclusive. In the meantime, Toni van Saikin noticed a malfunction in the purification mechanism and I remember saying that maybe these problems were premonitory signs. As if to prove me right, the sorting turbine didn't work in the main delivery meter and the water reserves headed for the discharge channel interflowed with those from the main feeding channel. In other words, the proceeds from the reserves went into the recuperated water and vice versa. You can imagine the loss. Result: the headwaters of the Blue Nile could not be tested.

That left the Ganges or the Mekong. Toni van Saikin and Stanley La Paz sought advice and reached the conclusion that the Ganges from Varanasi to the delta was out of the question because of the chlorine ...

Beat.

(Mr. Chairman, that should read, "because of the phosphorus," and not, "because of the chlorine ... ")

Everyone makes the correction.

((chuckling) There's no chlorine in the Ganges!)

... was out of the question because of the phosphorus. So we flew farther east to the Mekong, on the 21st of May. The rains in Asia were identical to those in the Sudan. When I say rains, I mean downpour, not showers. You have no idea of the rains. There's only one word for it: worse than the Deluge. By the second week, we expected Toni van Saikin to abandon the campsite. Instead, he decided we would set up operations at Prak-Kèk, not far from the border. It was courting catastrophe, in a region so far from the capital and so close to enemy territory, U.N. troops don't even venture there. Around mid-July, we sent the meteorologist, Stanley La Paz, back to the United States. Reason: the rain made him depressed. He wandered away from the camp more and more often. He said he couldn't stand the sight of the amputees, even though he plotted God knows what with them, and asked us for money more and more frequently so they could provide him with something he called a remedy. Terminating his contract entailed three weeks of administrative hassles.

There were other hitches, like the rains and the subsequent floods, complete with the appearance of eighteen-inch scorpions in the company of various protero-reptilians, daddy-long-legs that sting, huge spiders that transmit dengue fever, erysipelas,

coliform bacillus,
salmonellosis,
trichinosis,
bacterial dysentery,
malaria,
intestinal amoebiasis,
parasitosis,
ascaridiosis,
enteritis,
phlegmon,
erysipelas,
Pitt's syndrome,
whooping cough,
plague,
rabies and tetanus.

But the hypothesis to the effect that Toni van Saikin received a fatal bite is blurred by the fact that he was aware of the consequences and the dangers of the venom, as well as of the preventive measures. And the picture got grimmer day by day.

In the light of his death, we could only concur on failure. Ten days later, engineer Xu Sojen joined us at the campsite and concluded that we had to abandon everything on the spot and go home. The distance from inhabited areas and the weather conditions had made conversation, uh, conservation of the body impossible, and that's why we brought back some of his bones, to authenticate the facts, for identification purposes, and for the possibility of determining the cause of Toni van Saikin's death, since the fragments of his farewell letter were for the most part illegible, as mentioned earlier, despite repeated reading and re-reading. We searched everywhere but found nothing else. David Lenowski even considered at length a hypothesis suggesting a code obtained by replacing each letter with a number and each number with another letter, which produced nonsense and proved that this vague letter is, without a doubt, a farewell letter, thank you for your attention.

LLOYD MACURDY

Question, Mr. Chairman.

NIKOLS OSTWALD

Mr. Macurdy?

LLOYD MACURDY

What were the results obtained by the decoding?

RALPH PETERSON

As I said, the results were nothing more, nothing less than nonsense.

LLOYD MACURDY

Can you be more precise? Nonsense is relative. Mr. Lenowski, just what did you hope to obtain?

DAVID LENOWSKI

Toni van Saikin might have wanted to say something other than the sentences he left us.

JASON CASSILLY

And what did you find?

DAVID LENOWSKI

Words that don't exist.

LLOYD MACURDY

What words?

DAVID LENOWSKI

They don't exist.

LLOYD MACURDY

But you wrote them down?

DAVID LENOWSKI

Yes, but to no avail, we can't even pronounce them.
It was a hypothesis—a false expectation.

RALPH PETERSON

Mr. Chairman, I made a note of the results.

DAVID LENOWSKI

It's not worth it, Mr. Peterson.

RALPH PETERSON

Pure nonsense. "When you read these lines," for
instance, becomes approximately … "Swacpf xeqwu
niktgb egu nikpgu." You see. Are the members of this
inquiry convinced?

NIKOLS OSTWALD

Gentlemen, I must remind you that we have to
vacate this room by ten o'clock.

LLOYD MACURDY

You said … "Swacpf …" and how do you spell that?

NIKOLS OSTWALD

Order, gentlemen!

RALPH PETERSON
    Read it for yourself.

NIKOLS OSTWALD
    Order!

    Pause.

    You have our attention, Mr. Lenowski.

DAVID LENOWSKI
    Mr. Chairman …

    Pause.

DAVID LENOWSKI

I've read the fragments of Toni van Saikin's farewell
letter. Several barely legible pages, but one can
surmise that he was constantly reworking this letter.
At first glance, in the appendix of our report, it looks
like a traveller's diary, an unfinished diary, written in
longhand, an authentic document, the only lasting
souvenir of a sojourn "in this god-forsaken part of
the world," the part of the world he writes of.

When you read these lines …
When you read these lines, on this shore far from all
landmarks …
By the time you have read these lines …

We were used to seeing him design machines, draw
scale models, purification units. He was looking for
an alternative procedure. Our unit had been badly
damaged and we weren't surprised to see Toni van
Saikin isolate himself every evening. He wasn't very
talkative, and personally I had absolutely no desire to
know the outcome of his efforts. I knew that this
expedition bound to fail, no matter what.

Mr. Chairman …

Mr. Chairman, I have nothing to hide from you. Nor
do I have anything to reveal to you.

Concerning these fragments … I personally do not
believe that he was writing to us. We were there,
throughout the six months the expedition lasted. We
saw each other day after day. If he had had
something to say to us, he wouldn't have bothered to

write it. One tends to forget that behind these words is a man we know. As if this letter were not from him. One keeps harping on what is written. And since what is written has little to tell, and since it is unclear why there is so little to read, although he spent so much time writing … when one thinks of all those things that might have been found and which, at the very least, it would have been necessary to re-read …

As for this expedition … I admit I hardly know where to begin … Everything has a beginning, but … supposing, Mr. Chairman, that I were able to begin wherever I wanted, it wouldn't be much easier. I'd have to add the rest, one way or another … The water chambers, the cylinder, the nickel and cadmium batteries, the coral, the meccano structure, all that iron … The reports are there, in front of you …

Nobody in our immediate circle was particularly convinced about this expedition. When you go away for so long, so far, with an invention … it was our survival that we were taking with us over there, a unit to provide drinking water for foreign continents, a meccano set so we could sleep and take shelter from the rain.

Yes, to quote the expression used by my colleague, Ralph Peterson, it felt like the Deluge. The Deluge, but in slow motion. A period, that's it. Those grey layers in the atmosphere. A long period designed specifically to send all the necessary melancholy our way. From Khartoum to Phnom-Penh and from Phnom-Penh to Prak-Kèk, it rained. Rain followed us incessantly. Day and night. The mind and the body no longer work the same way when you're on the other side of the world, in rains so continuous you think you're in another life. Somewhere where there is no vegetation, no ground, no solid ground, you have been deported to a world of water, you are both inside and outside the water. It is impossible to interrogate us about what it was like living through those rains.

We were on the Blue Nile, upstream from Khartoum. Everything started to go wrong on the very first day. I saw that as a warning signal. The cylinder in the main turbine was tilted too much in relation to the spiral's axis. So we were filling the sorting chamber by hand, we had to spell each other. Day and night, Mr. Chairman. During his time off, he, the engineer, was always writing. We thought he was writing down his invention. What could be more natural for an inventor? And besides, he said it himself: I write to invent something.

Toni van Saikin cared a great deal about this expedition …
I …
Yes … as if it had to be …
A journey that becomes
a great gap in one's memory
if it fails …

Silence. Long silence.

NIKOLS OSTWALD
Could anything have led you to expect … that …

DAVID LENOWSKI

Expect? ... What should we have expected? To find him dead from one day to the next, because he was writing a letter? Why would we have deduced that he was going to die? ... If I were going to take my l ...

... Mr. Chairman, I wouldn't write about it to others.

When preparing these notes for my report ... I thought ... when a man writes a letter before ... a farewell letter before leaving ... he must go over his life, in terms of stages, of essential points, and it must be strange to think that you've reached the end ... already ... He begins by saying: "By the time you have read these lines ..." But just imagine the man who, over a period of months, takes more than twenty pages to rewrite the same sentence over and over, twenty pages to re-evaluate the introduction to the subject because he's not sure of the expression: when you read these lines, by the time you have read these lines ... As a result, he had to announce the outcome immediately, his death before all the rest, and that took him so many days, so many weeks, that one wonders if he really wanted to die so badly, after all.

JASON CASSILLY

(He had decided to die.)

NIKOLS OSTWALD

(Order!)

No. Nothing led us to expect it. This farewell letter, these excerpts? An accident, perhaps, that defies the precision of geology ... Look at the Blue Nile ... Stand in Khartoum and try to figure out whether it flows towards Memphis. It seems like an objective impossibility.

To RALPH PETERSON:

Pure nonsense!

Pause.

You have to be looking at a map and even then you're going to think that geographical maps, as precise as they are, are not telling you the truth. Something written there in print, and yet it's a lie.

To have expected that on that particular night ... Toni van Saikin would get up without anyone hearing him? Why? We found him, he was sitting up against one of the pylons. Our radio sets weren't working. We were far away. I was far away. It's hard to say exactly how long it took us to realize ...

Several days went by ...
I stood ...
Ten days went by, if I go by the reports, and I often went to stand beside him ... we were waiting for Xu Sojen.

I'd go and stand beside him, looking out at the Mekong Delta. At the river spilling out of its bed, preparing to enter the China Sea. It was around the week ... the last week in September, I had opened my notebook to the page marked the 22nd to jot

down my observations on the state of the world, and the rains. I remember writing that engineer Toni van Saikin was dead and that the universe was stable.
I ...
I thank you for your attention.

Pause.

NIKOLS OSTWALD

I have some questions.

His reports are topsy-turvy.

First of all, I would like to thank you. With the exception of a few details, and we'll get back to those in due time, everything seems in order. Mr. Lloyd Macurdy …

LLOYD MACURDY

Mr. Chairman?

NIKOLS OSTWALD

You submitted to this inquiry, along with a copy of your report, a copy of the paper written for the Geology Department last fall. If I am not mistaken, this paper constituted the final exam for the year? …

LLOYD MACURDY

Yes, it was an obligatory assignment in one of the lab courses.

NIKOLS OSTWALD

And the very same document was submitted to the National Research Center's annual competition?

LLOYD MACURDY

… If you like.

NIKOLS OSTWALD

What I would like is a precise answer.

LLOYD MACURDY

That depends upon what you mean.

NIKOLS OSTWALD

Was it the same document?

LLOYD MACURDY

Well, more or less.

NIKOLS OSTWALD

I have to be able to write either yes or no.

LLOYD MACURDY

Then write yes.

NIKOLS OSTWALD

So, it was your end of the year assignment that allowed you to win the National Research Center competition?

LLOYD MACURDY

... Yes.

NIKOLS OSTWALD

You don't seem too sure.

LLOYD MACURDY

Neither do you, Mr. Chairman. May I ask you why it is so important?

NIKOLS OSTWALD

It is not at all important. I am simply trying to get you to be precise.

LLOYD MACURDY

We submitted the integral version of our paper. We simply added the cost estimate and the specifications at the end. And, suddenly it comes back to me ... we changed the names of the rivers so the paper would meet the norm set by the National Center.

NIKOLS OSTWALD

Only the names of the rivers?

LLOYD MACURDY

And the names of the countries, of course!

NIKOLS OSTWALD

You were able, just like that, to change the geographical aspect of your paper without modifying the parameters of your unit?

LLOYD MACURDY

Inasmuch as we remained in tropical regions, there was no change in the scientific data.

NIKOLS OSTWALD

I see ... The Nile, the Mekong. What rivers were in your paper?

LLOYD MACURDY

The Blue Nile replaced the Nile. As for the Mekong, it ... just a minute, I have to think ... it was the St. Lawrence in Canada.

NIKOLS OSTWALD

But ... that's not a tropical river.

LLOYD MACURDY

But the Mekong is.

NIKOLS OSTWALD

You just said the scientific data were only applicable to tropical regions.

LLOYD MACURDY

That is correct—although certain rivers south of the equator contain residue which would have made it impossible for us to test our unit. Take the Ganges, for example.

NIKOLS OSTWALD

And the St. Lawrence doesn't contain any?

LLOYD MACURDY

As a matter of fact, it does, almost as much as the Danube.

NIKOLS OSTWALD

So why the St. Lawrence?

LLOYD MACURDY

For a very simple reason, Mr. Chairman. We needed to prove to the Department that Professor Déjanire never read our papers.

NIKOLS OSTWALD

The visiting professor? Why he's considered an expert …

LLOYD MACURDY

Because of his title of Field Marshall. But not for his pedagogical competence. Furthermore, he was repatriated to the Ivory Coast.

NIKOLS OSTWALD

He didn't read your assignments? What a scandal …

LLOYD MACURDY

He'd read two pages at the beginning and two pages at the end. The rest was simply too much for him.

He gave us an eighty. Twenty points a page. With a comment suggesting that we present the paper to the National Geological Research Center competition. Which we did, once it was corrected.

Beat.

Any other questions?

NIKOLS OSTWALD

Yes, regarding the conclusion in your report. You enumerate the causes which explain, in your opinion, the failure of this expedition. The malfunction in the unit, the extent of the rainfall, the floods … You do not include Toni van Saikin's death among these causes. On the contrary, you claim he died because the expedition was bound to fail.

LLOYD MACURDY

I add that that is merely a hypothesis.

NIKOLS OSTWALD

You say, and I quote: "I think, on the contrary, that Toni van Saikin died because this expedition was in any case bound to fail." Do you really believe that Toni van Saikin could have taken his own life?

LLOYD MACURDY

Yes, I do.

NIKOLS OSTWALD

May I ask you why?

LLOYD MACURDY

Because it's obvious.

NIKOLS OSTWALD

Then it's not a hypothesis.

LLOYD MACURDY

Mr. Chairman, one doesn't simply die, just like that, of nothing. He was in perfect health. I have the results of our medical examinations here. Read them for yourself. We were all in perfect health.

NIKOLS OSTWALD

Couldn't he have caught some disease over there?

LLOYD MACURDY

Why him and not us?

NIKOLS OSTWALD

So you attribute the causes of the failure to a mechanical breakdown.

LLOYD MACURDY

Yes, for the most part. The sorting turbine was not working.

JASON CASSILLY

Wrong! It was working.

LLOYD MACURDY

You tried to repair it yourself!

JASON CASSILLY

It was the main cylinder that was defective.

LLOYD MACURDY

But one couldn't work without the other. We're saying the same thing!

JASON CASSILLY

No, we're not, not exactly. I'm even afraid I must contradict you slightly.

NIKOLS OSTWALD

Gentlemen …

JASON CASSILLY

I would like to submit a few rectifications to this inquiry. My colleague does not seem know the difference between a sorting turbine and a single-cylinder densifier. It's obvious that his professor didn't read his assignments very often.

LLOYD MACURDY

The cylinders work on the same hydraulic principles within the same unit.

JASON CASSILLY

Yes, perhaps, but not at the same speed! Which means there's a loss of energy.

NIKOLS OSTWALD

Gentlemen, please …

JASON CASSILLY

And a terrible loss of time!

NIKOLS OSTWALD

Mr. Cassilly …

JASON CASSILLY

I can give you an example: take an atom of iron and an atom of hydrogen. Everyone knows that iron is atomically more complex than hydrogen. Within the strict realm of particle physics, it certainly has to be said that—

LLOYD MACURDY

Mr. Cassilly, the question cannot be seen in terms of particle physics.

JASON CASSILLY

Then exactly what are we talking about?

NIKOLS OSTWALD

For the time being, I would like you to leave the mechanical aspect aside. If necessary, I shall consult the reports. They are very explicit on this point.

JASON CASSILLY

You will find contradictions.

NIKOLS OSTWALD

I have noted the contradictions.

LLOYD MACURDY

Between who and who?

NIKOLS OSTWALD

It doesn't really matter. There are contradictions within the same reports.

RALPH PETERSON

The names of insects, perhaps, Mr. Chairman?

NIKOLS OSTWALD

I do not wish to discuss insects. Or mechanics. Cylinders, spirals …

On these matters, I shall refer to your report, Mr. Cassilly. I wish, however, that you were as precise concerning all the rest.

JASON CASSILLY

I made an effort to be as precise as possible.

NIKOLS OSTWALD

I'm talking about all the reports. Not one of you is capable of placing the events in the same chronological order. You all become vague when it comes to dates. Mr. Lenowski sets Toni van Saikin's death around the 22nd of September. Yet we sent engineer Xu Sojen to Cambodia on September 8th. If we count the ten days between the death of the former and the arrival of the latter, that takes us back to the end of August. You tell me you had lost all sense of time. That is why I say you are not precise. This inquiry is investigating the causes of a failure, and primarily, the causes of a man's death.

JASON CASSILLY

He had decided to die.

NIKOLS OSTWALD

I have made note of that. But that is not sufficient. I have more than enough information to complete the file on the mechanical breakdown of the unit. You have spoken at length about the unfavourable conditions, I have made note of the essential. The rains, the floods, and the other points on which you all agree. But when I ask the question, "Why did Toni van Saikin die in the course of this expedition?"

you reply and I quote: "He had decided to die."
Gentlemen, I would like you to go further than that.

LLOYD MACURDY

Toni van Saikin is no longer here to explain.

NIKOLS OSTWALD

That is precisely why we are here.

JASON CASSILLY

We can hardly speak for him.

LLOYD MACURDY

Especially since he wasn't very talkative himself.

NIKOLS OSTWALD

But he must have talked to you occasionally!

LLOYD MACURDY

Oh, he talked to us, about water tanks, gas, steam, pressurized methane, dry rocks …

RALPH PETERSON

… Cylinders, spirals …

NIKOLS OSTWALD

I know. He talked about things you could understand. And I suppose you responded with energy, combustibles, water reserves … Nevertheless, I would like someone to tell me who Toni van Saikin was, I would like to have a portrait of the man.

LLOYD MACURDY

A portrait? …

NIKOLS OSTWALD

I mean, in the broadest sense.

JASON CASSILLY

I see. A fact sheet.

RALPH PETERSON

There's this, along with a photograph, in his file.

THE GEOLOGISTS

Portrait of Toni van Saikin. Sex: male. Age: twenty-nine. Height: five foot eleven. B.P.: 120 over 80. Cholesterol: eighty-eight point four. Hemoglobin: twelve. Body type: ectomorph. White blood cell count: slight, insignificant leukocytosis. Blood type: AB positive. Lungs: area of hyperdensity, signs of parenchymatous scar tissue. Munchausen's syndrome: insufficient data. Urinalysis: potassium: four point two; no proteins, no casts; urinary M.H.P.G.: slightly decreased. Fasting blood iron: normal, calcium: 10 mg per cent. Hearing: ninety-eight per cent; ADN zero point zero zero zero nine …

NIKOLS OSTWALD

I mean, in the broadest sense!

JASON CASSILLY

Myopia: point zero zero five.

LLOYD MACURDY

Babinski reflex: normal. Impeccable set of teeth.

RALPH PETERSON

No medical problems.

LLOYD MACURDY

He had had three vaccinations.

RALPH PETERSON

Including one for paludism.

JASON CASSILLY

One says "against."

NIKOLS OSTWALD

So, Toni van Saikin is in perfect health at the time of his departure. He is in perfect health in Khartoum. Three months later in Phnom-Penh, he is still in perfect health. And then … and then … he dies. How is this possible? Answer: he had decided to die. Answer: he was writing a farewell letter. For how long? We don't really know. I hope you'll forgive the brutality of my question, but you are forcing me to ask it. Could any one of you have had a vested interest in seeing engineer Toni van Saikin die in the course of this expedition?

Silence.

JASON CASSILLY

No one, obviously. On the contrary. We all ran the risk of finding ourselves stuck there. Communication between Phnom-Penh and Minneapolis had been cut off.

NIKOLS OSTWALD

You knew that?

JASON CASSILLY

We realized it when we wanted to notify you of his death.

NIKOLS OSTWALD

But had anyone tried to communicate with the university before his death?

LLOYD MACURDY

We had thought of doing it, but we thought we'd be able to find a solution on our own.

NIKOLS OSTWALD

Even though everyone was convinced that this expedition was going to fail from the outset?

JASON CASSILLY

Everyone except Toni van Saikin.

NIKOLS OSTWALD

Not a single telegram? Nothing to inform us that something was wrong?

LLOYD MACURDY

We preferred to wait.

NIKOLS OSTWALD

Wait for what? Sunny weather?

LLOYD MACURDY

For Toni to decide. For everything to fall into place. And besides, we would have had to get to Phnom-Penh to send a telegram—it was an eight-hour walk. In a country where every step can trigger a mine field in the middle of the jungle. A country of amputees. The most dangerous country in the world with the most land mines. The roads are impossible, the corpses along the banks of the rivers would discourage anyone from trying to cross them.

NIKOLS OSTWALD

And you knew all that without having attempted the journey?

LLOYD MACURDY

People told us.

NIKOLS OSTWALD

In what language did these people tell you this?

LLOYD MACURDY

God, you've got me there. Probably in Cambodian, but we understood their gestures. And we just had to take one look at them. They trekked through mud up to their knees, sometimes up to the waist. And the looks of terror on their faces when they saw us. We thought it was epilepsy, but it wasn't. It was terror.

RALPH PETERSON

Xu Sojen spoke Cambodian with them.

NIKOLS OSTWALD

I'm talking about before that, well before his arrival. I'm talking about before Toni van Saikin's death. There's no way you could have known everything you're telling me now at the time of your arrival in Cambodia. Toni van Saikin died in September, you claim. I'm talking about June. All you know is that the expedition was going to fail. Gentlemen, I would like you to go further than that. Did anyone try to get in touch with the university before September?

JASON CASSILLY

No, since the radio set wasn't working.

NIKOLS OSTWALD

So someone had tried?

LLOYD MACURDY

No. Since the radio set wasn't working, how many times do we have to tell you.

NIKOLS OSTWALD

But someone had to try to use the radio set in order to discover that it wasn't working.

JASON CASSILLY

Listen, it wasn't working. It wasn't worth trying!

Long silence. Tension.

NIKOLS OSTWALD

Gentlemen, I …

RALPH PETERSON

Mr. Chairman, we just knew it, period.

NIKOLS OSTWALD

One can't know that an object is out of order without having previously tested it.

RALPH PETERSON

Then someone must have tested it.

NIKOLS OSTWALD

Exactly. And I would like to know who.

RALPH PETERSON

Well … one of us.

NIKOLS OSTWALD

I realize that! But which one?

LLOYD MACURDY
One of us.

NIKOLS OSTWALD
WHO?

LLOYD MACURDY
My god, is it really that important?

NIKOLS OSTWALD
It's crucial. I have to report specifics.

DAVID LENOWSKI
Write down that it was me.

NIKOLS OSTWALD
Ah? … So … it was you?

DAVID LENOWSKI
Yes, Mr. Chairman.

NIKOLS OSTWALD
But … but why be so obstinate? Why not say so?

DAVID LENOWSKI
I just said so.

NIKOLS OSTWALD
When I ask a question, Gentlemen …

JASON CASSILLY
Alright then, write down that it was me.

NIKOLS OSTWALD
But I asked you …

LLOYD MACURDY

Alright, so it was me, you may as well know it was me.

RALPH PETERSON

You know, Mr. Chairman. You should write that it was everyone and the inquiry will be satisfied.

Beat. NIKOLS OSTWALD is writing.

NIKOLS OSTWALD

Should I write: "because of the rain?"

JASON CASSILLY

Basically, yes. The electromagnetic or Hertz waves operate at a frequency which can be modified by any type of vibration or deformation, if you prefer, and their amplitude is a periodic function of variables in time and space, and consequently of variables in the weather. Something which must be taken into consideration from the outset is that tropical rains can cause interference—in this case one refers to stationary waves—brought about by two sources with the same periodic frequency and the same force in opposite phases …

NIKOLS OSTWALD

That will do, Mr. Cassilly, I've made a note of that.

JASON CASSILLY

Yes, but it might be wrong, because there is another hypothesis.

NIKOLS OSTWALD

I'll get back to you for the details. Thank you.

JASON CASSILLY

At any rate, the radio set was not working, we knew it, and we even knew why.

NIKOLS OSTWALD

Thank you. Mr. Cassilly, based on your report, I assume that you knew engineer Toni van Saikin quite well?

JASON CASSILLY

I had a great deal of respect for him.

NIKOLS OSTWALD

One can have a great deal of respect for someone one doesn't know.

JASON CASSILLY

I think we have more respect for people we know.

NIKOLS OSTWALD

So you knew Toni van Saikin well?

JASON CASSILLY

That depends upon what you mean by well.

NIKOLS OSTWALD

I would like you to answer yes or no.

JASON CASSILLY

If I answered no, I would be lying to you.

NIKOLS OSTWALD

Then you did know him well.

JASON CASSILLY

In one sense.

NIKOLS OSTWALD

(*unruffled*) In what sense?

JASON CASSILLY

He was not someone you got to know easily.

NIKOLS OSTWALD

Meaning?

JASON CASSILLY

He wasn't very talkative. He was strange.

NIKOLS OSTWALD

Could you go further than that?

JASON CASSILLY

He was strange.

Beat.

NIKOLS OSTWALD

Fine … It seems to me, once again based on your report, that you are very critical of what you call Toni van Saikin's "idealistic" side.

JASON CASSILLY

And even then, I'm putting on my velvet gloves.

NIKOLS OSTWALD

So you had a great deal of respect for him, but nevertheless …

JASON CASSILLY

I had a great deal of respect for his intelligence. He was a remarkable person on that level.

NIKOLS OSTWALD

You do however criticize him for—

JASON CASSILLY

I criticize him for nothing. I simply state a fact, that's
all. Toni van Saikin denied the obvious. In the face of
reality, he persevered, in the name of God knows
what conviction. An irrational faith that proved
nothing and claimed to be all-encompassing. And we
saw where it led.

NIKOLS OSTWALD

So you too were convinced that this expedition was
bound to fail?

JASON CASSILLY

Mr. Chairman, if you like, I could show you, using
drawings, how a single-cylinder turbine works. A
child could understand—as long as the explanation
was clear—and anyone who was shown where our
unit had broken down would be convinced that the
expedition could not help but fail. Anyone except
Toni van Saikin.

NIKOLS OSTWALD

In the days preceding his death ... I hope you'll
forgive me for insisting ... no one noticed ...
anything? ... Any signs?

RALPH PETERSON

He was the same as usual.

NIKOLS OSTWALD

And how was that?

LLOYD MACURDY

The same as usual. He was strange.

NIKOLS OSTWALD

Meaning?

JASON CASSILLY

Toni van Saikin was a strange man.

NIKOLS OSTWALD

Just what do you mean? I'd like you to go further than that.

LLOYD MACURDY

He was strange.

NIKOLS OSTWALD

In what way was he strange?

THE GEOLOGISTS

…

NIKOLS OSTWALD

His attitude? His behaviour?

THE GEOLOGISTS

No.

NIKOLS OSTWALD

His way of relating to you? Was he strange in what he had to say?

LLOYD MACURDY

No.

RALPH PETERSON

What he said made sense.

NIKOLS OSTWALD

So?

THE GEOLOGISTS

He was strange.

NIKOLS OSTWALD

Gentlemen, go further than that. I can't write that
Toni van Saikin died because he was ...

JASON CASSILLY

Listen, he was strange. He spent hours talking with
Stanley La Paz, the meteorologist. Toni must have
realized that Stanley wasn't well. All of us had
realized it. But he had to crack up.

LLOYD MACURDY

I can still hear him screaming with anxiety, begging
us to send for healers and bonzes.

DAVID LENOWSKI

He wanted us to take him to Vientiane so we could
cure him with naja elixirs made from whole cobras
steeped in alcohol. So we could inject roundworms
under his skin. And cover his eyes with a poultice of
crushed frogs. We'd ask him: "Stanley, what's the
weather for tomorrow?" And he'd reply that he
forecast clearing over the Arno, while demanding
that we make an incision in his leg to draw the
parasites out of his blood.

JASON CASSILLY

We had asked Toni van Saikin to authorize Stanley's
return as early as our second week in Khartoum.

LLOYD MACURDY

But Toni told us we had to wait.

JASON CASSILLY

Wait!

RALPH PETERSON

We had to move on.

JASON CASSILLY

We always had to move on. The Sudan, Ethiopia, even India, it was never far enough! Stanley La Paz is the one we should have followed. Mr. Chairman, Toni van Saikin was a strange man.

LLOYD MACURDY

We were in the middle of the jungle and he was talking about collaborating with the Good Will Workers to help flood victims, and victims of other catastrophes. He started hoarding aspirin, inventing serums and hypertonic pads. All that was costly and we had no money. But that didn't stop him! A herb growing in the mud sent him into a morbid meditation on Gods knows what and suddenly it was imperative that we advise Washington.

RALPH PETERSON

Pure nonsense. While we were taking turns filling the sorter by hand, Mr. Chairman, Toni van Saikin was studying botany. He was interested in angiospermous gramineous plants. He had discovered a cure for cancer. Just like on television. If you're not happy with the word "strange," just write that he was neurasthenic, cyclothymic, write that he was crazy.

NIKOLS OSTWALD

But one doesn't die of that, Mr. Peterson.

LLOYD MACURDY

And yet!

RALPH PETERSON

And yet, indeed! Read for yourself: "*When you read these lines ...*"

LLOYD MACURDY

"*By the time you have read these lines ...*"

RALPH PETERSON

Three times! Five times! Eight times! To say nothing of the rest, the body of the letter, and the conclusion. And the signature!

JASON CASSILLY

You know, it's true. There's no signature.

LLOYD MACURDY

But it's his handwriting.

NIKOLS OSTWALD

This farewell letter ...

JASON CASSILLY

Can one really speak of a letter?

LLOYD MACURDY

What should one speak of then?

NIKOLS OSTWALD

Please, Gentlemen ...

DAVID LENOWSKI

He began it over and over again …

NIKOLS OSTWALD

Order!

JASON CASSILLY

Go further than that!

RALPH PETERSON

Read for yourself!

DAVID LENOWSKI

Over and over again. Xu Sojen claims he was writing
without thinking of anyone in particular. A letter to
no one. Like talking out loud when you're all alone.

RALPH PETERSON

Only madmen talk to themselves.

DAVID LENOWSKI

He wanted to die. He must have never finished this
letter.

JASON CASSILLY

It can't be called a letter if he never finished it. A
letter becomes valid once one has clearly ceased to
think of starting it over.

RALPH PETERSON

Try to follow my logic: he was always starting it over,
so he never got around to finishing it. But since
everyone knows that Toni van Saikin wanted to die,
what he really cared about finishing, when you get
right down to it, was his life.

JASON CASSILLY

How can you call that logic?

RALPH PETERSON

It was either his letter or his life.

DAVID LENOWSKI

You mean, he would have finished it in order to survive? But in that case, the letter wouldn't have said the same thing?

RALPH PETERSON

That's right, the letter would have lied.

DAVID LENOWSKI

An impossible letter. The mere fact that it exists means it says the opposite.

RALPH PETERSON

Even if it says nothing at all.

LLOYD MACURDY

I don't follow you there, Mr. Peterson.

RALPH PETERSON

At any rate, it says very little, read for yourself.

JASON CASSILLY

How do you call that, Mr. Peterson, pure nothingness?

RALPH PETERSON

Pure nonsense!

NIKOLS OSTWALD

Gentlemen ... this letter ...

JASON CASSILLY

I don't think we can call it a letter. It isn't signed. Legally, it's worthless.

LLOYD MACURDY

Hah! I like to know what it would be worth if it were signed!

JASON CASSILLY

Exactly what are talking about? These are only fragments. Fragments that repeat themselves. Eight fragments that bear witness to a single sentence. For a letter to be valid, we have to be able to read more than that, let's say, I don't know, at least two-thirds!

RALPH PETERSON

I would say at least half.

NIKOLS OSTWALD

Gentlemen, please …

LLOYD MACURDY

Even a quarter would give us an idea …

RALPH PETERSON

With or without a post-scriptum?

The geologists laugh hilariously. The Chairman raises his voice.

NIKOLS OSTWALD

Order!

RALPH PETERSON

Go further!

LLOYD MACURDY

Read for yourself!

NIKOLS OSTWALD

Silence!

Calm.

JASON CASSILLY

Question, Mr. Chairman?

NIKOLS OSTWALD

Back to your reports, please. Back to your reports. Jason Cassilly, you say and I quote: "Toni van Saikin never wrote anything that remotely resembled scientific notes or observations." That's on page seventeen of your report. Do you still maintain that Toni van Saikin spent his evenings composing a farewell letter of which we now possess only the beginning of three sentences?

JASON CASSILLY

That is correct, Mr. Chairman.

NIKOLS OSTWALD

David Lenowski, on page one of your report, you say and I quote: "He was trying to find an alternative procedure." Farther on, you claim that you thought he was writing down his invention. Isn't that what you said?

DAVID LENOWSKI

Maybe.

NIKOLS OSTWALD

Maybe yes?

DAVID LENOWSKI

Yes.

NIKOLS OSTWALD

Don't you find, Mr. Cassilly, that your report contradicts what Mr. Lenowski claims.

JASON CASSILLY

With all due respect to Mr. Lenowski—

NIKOLS OSTWALD

Might Toni van Saikin have written about the disappointing results of your experiments, attributing the failure to certain mistakes for which some of you could have been responsible?

JASON CASSILLY

What are you trying to insinuate? That he was attempting to blame his colleagues?

NIKOLS OSTWALD

Were these notes scientific observations, or simply the ranting and raving of a man who had, according to your report, "decided to die?"

JASON CASSILLY

You are insinuating, Mr. Chairman.

NIKOLS OSTWALD

You are dodging, Mr. Cassilly.

RALPH PETERSON

Pardon me, but why do you find the brilliant Mr. Cassilly's interpretation, unlike that of Mr. Lenowski, the poet in the group, so convincing that you think the most precise of the four of us is not telling the truth in his report?

NIKOLS OSTWALD

In the appendix to your report, Mr. Peterson, I believe you included some photographs?

RALPH PETERSON

That's right. Some photographs taken in Khartoum.

NIKOLS OSTWALD

Who is that man in the background?

RALPH PETERSON

That's Jason Cassilly.

NIKOLS OSTWALD

(to JASON CASSILLY) Really? I never would have recognized you!

JASON CASSILLY

That's understandable: because of the particularly bright sun in Khartoum, infra-red rays can be emitted at a certain temperature and the atmosphere they create—although invisible even with a telescope—is comparable to a kind of corridor through space, where imbricated universes, reputed to have the same properties as black holes, emit x-rays to which the negative of this photo was presumably sensitive. That's why it looks as if I have purple hair.

NIKOLS OSTWALD

Speaking of this photograph, Mr. Cassilly ... I can't help but notice that the sun was shining that day?

JASON CASSILLY

That's a fact.

NIKOLS OSTWALD

And yet all your reports state unanimously that it rained without letup, both in the Sudan and in Cambodia.

JASON CASSILLY

So?

NIKOLS OSTWALD

So ... did it rain without letup or did it rain intermittently?

JASON CASSILLY

I see. We were lacking in precision once again. But I am categorical, Mr. President. It rained constantly.

NIKOLS OSTWALD

Every day? For all six months?

JASON CASSILLY

It rained constantly.

NIKOLS OSTWALD

Except for the day of the photograph ...

JASON CASSILLY

It rained that day, too.

NIKOLS OSTWALD

I'm sorry to insist.

JASON CASSILLY

I'm telling you it was constantly raining.

NIKOLS OSTWALD

But this photograph proves that it was sunny, if only for one minute. You must remember that moment.

JASON CASSILLY

I don't remember it.

Beat.

NIKOLS OSTWALD

(brusquely) Who took this photograph?

THE GEOLOGISTS

...

NIKOLS OSTWALD

Who took this photograph? It didn't take itself? ... Was it you, Mr. Macurdy?

LLOYD MACURDY

No, since I'm in it.

NIKOLS OSTWALD

Where are you?

LLOYD MACURDY

There on the left. Just a minute. On the right.

NIKOLS OSTWALD

Is that you?

RALPH PETERSON

It's because of the black hole. Everyone's hair is purple.

NIKOLS OSTWALD

And is that you, on the left, Mr. Peterson?

RALPH PETERSON
    No. That's ... wait—that's an international aid
    worker.

NIKOLS OSTWALD
    And who is that?

RALPH PETERSON
    That's me. And that's Stanley La Paz, here.

NIKOLS OSTWALD
    That's not Mr. Lenowski?

DAVID LENOWSKI
    No, it's Stanley La Paz.

NIKOLS OSTWALD
    Then you're missing, Mr. Lenowski.

DAVID LENOWSKI
    Of course, since I was behind the lens.

NIKOLS OSTWALD
    Then you were the one who took this photograph?

DAVID LENOWSKI
    Yes, it was me.

NIKOLS OSTWALD
    But that's what I was asking! Why didn't you answer?

DAVID LENOWSKI
    I just answered you: it was me.

NIKOLS OSTWALD
    Mr. Lenowski, what was the weather like that day?

DAVID LENOWSKI

It was raining.

NIKOLS OSTWALD

You're not going to try to tell me it's raining in this photograph?

DAVID LENOWSKI studies the photograph.

DAVID LENOWSKI

No, you're right.

NIKOLS OSTWALD

So it was sunny that day.

DAVID LENOWSKI

No, Mr. Chairman. It was raining.

NIKOLS OSTWALD

But you admit yourself that the sun is shining in this photograph?

DAVID LENOWSKI

From there to admitting that it was sunny that day … Listen, I don't want to contradict you, but I just can't remember.

NIKOLS OSTWALD

I don't enjoy having people make fun of me!

LLOYD MACURDY

Mr. Chairman, there are four of us here telling you it was raining that day.

NIKOLS OSTWALD

But your colleague is holding a document which constitutes indisputable proof to the contrary.

RALPH PETERSON

It was raining. You have our word for it.

NIKOLS OSTWALD

Try to remember more clearly.

JASON CASSILLY

(to LLOYD MACURDY) How about you?

LLOYD MACURDY

No. *(to RALPH PETERSON)* What about you?

RALPH PETERSON

Me neither.

NIKOLS OSTWALD

A man died in the course of this expedition. You tell me that a man died in the course of this expedition. But there are many details in your reports which you do not agree upon. Gentlemen, I have my doubts. You refuse to tell the truth. You deny the facts. And you reply: "He died because it's obvious." And just what is obvious? What good is the evidence? It was raining? But this photograph.

Beat.

An expedition takes place in the Sudan and in Cambodia. Financed by the State. On the basis of a paper which was not even supervised. An obligatory assignment. Which contained incongruities. Perhaps even serious mistakes. The jury is composed of professors from all disciplines, but most of them are economists. They're there to finance the projects. They receive over a hundred proposals every year. It is unrealistic to think that they can read them all carefully. Let's say you were lucky, at first, gentlemen.

You arrive in Khartoum. A mechanical breakdown, of which no one here was advised, jeopardizes the experiment. Only two weeks have gone by and all of you recognize that the expedition is bound to fail. It might not have been superfluous for us to know about it. But, oh, no. The radio set wasn't working. How did you know that? It doesn't matter, we knew it. Who had tested it? Just write that it was everyone.

A month later, or a month and a half later, time is not very important, furthermore you have all lost all sense of time, you change the itinerary. Once again, no one here is informed. An impulse. I ask you: Why? Answer: He was strange. Question: And this farewell letter? Answer: In either case, it would have lied. Answer: Read for yourself. It's pure nonsense, Mr. Peterson. It's sunny in the photograph, but it was raining when Mr. Lenowski took it. It's a miracle.

And the meteorologist? ... What did you do with him? A nervous breakdown, you claim? An ancient illness caused by superstitions? Could that man have told this inquiry what the weather was like in Khartoum? Gentlemen, that man returned home without our knowing it. And once again, I have nothing but your word for it. And what if this is not the only lie? A man died. Or so we are told. Why? That's not very important. He died, what more do you want to know? A man died. I ask you why. Why did you watch him die? Why this silence? Why not say why?

DAVID LENOWSKI

We were far away. Now that we're back, it seems even farther away.

NIKOLS OSTWALD

He was strange? And how about you, what were you?

DAVID LENOWSKI

It's easy to say: it's on the other side of the world. But it seemed so far away to me, it's as if we had changed worlds.

NIKOLS OSTWALD

Mr. Macurdy … Mr. Cassilly … Mr. Peterson … Mr. Lenowski … did one of you kill engineer Toni van Saikin?

THE GEOLOGISTS

…

NIKOLS OSTWALD

I am not asking for reasons. If there are any, I don't even want to know them at this point. After all, if one can die without reason, one must be able to assassinate without reason? …

RALPH PETERSON

In other words, all of us must have become … neurasthenic, cyclothymic, crazy! But I don't believe that Toni van Saikin died because someone killed him. He died because he wanted to die.

NIKOLS OSTWALD

Did he ever tell you that?

LLOYD MACURDY

No, Mr. Chairman. He did better than that. He wrote it. He left us fragments of his farewell letter and we read them.

NIKOLS OSTWALD

But previously, no one had any way of knowing. It's written clearly in your reports: "We didn't know." Read for yourselves.

JASON CASSILLY

We supposedly killed a man because we had no way of knowing that he wanted to die! Question, Mr. Chairman: If we had known, would we have done it? After all, if he had no reason for wanting to die, weren't we right in killing him? And, furthermore, without reason?

DAVID LENOWSKI

But ... this is not an inquiry, it's a trial! Go ahead, Mr. Chairman. Accuse us.

Beat.

(Accuse me.)

LLOYD MACURDY

And why couldn't he have taken his own life? Isn't that quite normal when someone wants to die?

NIKOLS OSTWALD

True ... Quite true ... It's a hypothesis. So, Mr. Macurdy ... how? How might he have taken his own life?

LLOYD MACURDY

I wasn't there. I didn't see a thing.

NIKOLS OSTWALD

Yes, you were there.

LLOYD MACURDY

We discovered his body after he was already dead.

NIKOLS OSTWALD

Who discovered it first?

THE GEOLOGISTS

...

NIKOLS OSTWALD

Was it you, Mr. Lenowski?

DAVID LENOWSKI

(indignant) Why me?

NIKOLS OSTWALD

I'm simply asking.

DAVID LENOWSKI

It wasn't me. Someone else saw him before me. When I went to tell them Toni was dead, I realized that they all knew it. No surprise, no panic, just embarrassed looks. Everyone knew it, Mr. Chairman, everyone had seen him, but no one had said it yet. And a man can be dead, but he never is definitely dead until someone can say it. Otherwise, it doesn't count. I think they were trying to prolong his life by not saying that he was dead.

NIKOLS OSTWALD

So you were the one who said it first?

DAVID LENOWSKI

I don't know any more. I don't think so. At first, I acted like them. I didn't say it.

NIKOLS OSTWALD

But afterwards? … In the hours, the days that followed?

DAVID LENOWSKI

Perhaps. But I don't have to answer that question.

NIKOLS OSTWALD

Pardon me?

DAVID LENOWSKI

I don't have to submit myself to this kind of interrogation.

NIKOLS OSTWALD

You are required to answer all the ques—

DAVID LENOWSKI

(cutting him off, nervously) That's what I meant, Mr. Chairman! This is a trial! And I am being accused!

JASON CASSILLY

I think the true intentions of this inquiry have been disguised.

LLOYD MACURDY

I share that opinion. In fact, I've had that feeling from the very beginning.

RALPH PETERSON

This is very serious, Mr. Chairman. We enter this room as honest citizens, and suddenly we walk out looking like murderers.

NIKOLS OSTWALD

Did you say "murderers?"

LLOYD MACURDY

Absolutely. Try to pin a murder on us! Make us feel guilty! Question, Mr. Chairman!

DAVID LENOWSKI

And we've being playing along with it! Who discovered his body first? Shall we show you our fingerprints!

THE GEOLOGISTS

Question, Mr. Chairman!

NIKOLS OSTWALD

(writing) "No one … discovered … his … body … first … Everyone … discovered … it … second. They … all … arrived … at the same time … with the result … that … no one … arrived … first. Why? … For … no … reason … Mr. Chairman … In Cambodia … people … die … for no reason."

Beat.

Madam?

CARLA VAN SAIKIN

Mr. Chairman?

NIKOLS OSTWALD

Another hypothesis. Let us suppose that the man had little time left to live. Cancer. A tumour. Or simply some congenital weakness in his body. An apparently benign problem, without symptoms, but one that could become fatal if the man were exposed for an extended period of time to a strange environment? … But these medical tests show that he was in perfect health. Mrs. Carla van Saikin, do you admit to having signed the medical reports for all the members of the team, including your husband's report?

CARLA VAN SAIKIN

Yes, I do, Mr. Chairman.

NIKOLS OSTWALD

Do you still maintain that your husband was in perfect health?

Silence, then:

CARLA VAN SAIKIN

Nothing could have prevented him from undertaking this expedition.

NIKOLS OSTWALD

It was that important to him?

CARLA VAN SAIKIN

Yes, Mr. Chairman. It was his whole life.

NIKOLS OSTWALD

Thank you.

Beat.

You see, Gentlemen. But, of course, that too is just another hypothesis. Since we have these fragments.

DAVID LENOWSKI

He might have written without realizing.

LLOYD MACURDY

There's also the possibility of an accident. The meccano structure was listing. To set it straight, we had to climb …

RALPH PETERSON

He might have slipped, fallen wrong …

DAVID LENOWSKI

Exhaustion …

LLOYD MACURDY

He might have hit his head on one of the pylons …

JASON CASSILLY

Question, Mr. Chairman.

RALPH PETERSON

There was the quicksand.

DAVID LENOWSKI

He might have called out for help, but with the noise of the rain … worse than silence …

LLOYD MACURDY

Go on, Mr. Peterson …

RALPH PETERSON

> There were the floods. And now that I think of it ...
> those peasants ... those foreigners ...

LLOYD MACURDY

> It's true, they were constantly spying on us!

RALPH PETERSON

> Those people are capable of having killed him.
> They're so different from us, they obey impulses ...

JASON CASSILLY

> They're xenophobic. Their territory threatened.

DAVID LENOWSKI

> But wouldn't he have screamed?

THE GEOLOGISTS

> Question, Mr. Chairman!

DAVID LENOWSKI

> With the noise of the rain, worse than silence ...

THE GEOLOGISTS

> Question, Mr. Chairman!

DAVID LENOWSKI

> ... silence ...

THE GEOLOGISTS

> Go on!

DAVID LENOWSKI

> A silent ship passes, so distant ...

THE GEOLOGISTS

> Question, Mr. Chairman!

DAVID LENOWSKI
    … so silent …

THE GEOLOGISTS
    Question, Mr. Chairman!

II

Ebrié Lagoon

CARLA VAN SAIKIN

They brought his bones back from the Mekong. In the final analysis, he was properly identified. Yes, it's him, yes, that's his sternum.

"Your husband, Toni van Saikin, died in the course of the expedition and here is the proof."

That's something he and I had in common: this enormous love, this passion for precision. Just as he was about to leave, I said to him: "The alluvium of these rivers contains natural properties I would like to analyse, I'd like to reduce them to a pure state, anyway, you'll see for yourself, and you'll write me ..." Our last words! Unless you can hear me now and these words count. Now is when we really part. I never would've thought that you'd return for me to say goodbye to your bones. I hate you. You smell of death. The damp smell of dead things. I'd like to take these objects and wash them in running water, it would make you seem dead for a longer time. Me, Carla, alive, and you, dead, gone forever ...

And yet, I've seen three others since. A highway accident, a case of poisoning and a third one, I forget ... All three around five o'clock in the morning, almost at the same time, as if they had arranged it. I was alone in the emergency ward. But I stayed calm. Ten more could have come in, as long as they were all that silent.

I saw the sun rise behind the ambulances. And I went over the day ahead of me. Here it is, six o'clock.

Six o'clock, Toni, you're going to be late, you have to be at the university by seven.

Our life started before daybreak and we were dead by five-thirty in the afternoon. You promised me Barcelona as consolation for Cambodia.

Bright sunshine over the city today. In a little while, I'll go back to the hospital. Two appointments yesterday afternoon, an interview with a young intern, I couldn't sleep as usual, despite the Halcion, and I have an operation this morning. A woman in her fifties, I'm going to take out her ... Just what am I going to take out? What's wrong with her? Is it her upper lobe or the alveola? I'd better find out. I haven't gone over my appointments carefully and I can't remember. Partial ablation of the lung ... left or right? Cancer or a tumour? A pneumonectomy or a thoracoplasty?

Such a beautiful day! ... Did you see the sun? Look at them. I put them near the window ... in a little while, some men are coming, they're going to pick them up and take you away—you certainly will have travelled a lot—but in the meantime, look, there they are in a ray of today's wonderful sun, you won't feel so cold ...

Now I remember: a thoracoplasty. Poor woman, if she has tuberculosis and I operate on her for cancer, she'll suffer unnecessarily, and she's suffering enough as is ...

Tomorrow your sternum will be warm and safe on its huge pillow inside the bronze box. They said there's going to be quite a crowd. They're going to

announce that the new wing of the Science Building
will be named after you. An important day, let's hope
the weather will be this nice.

I wonder what the rest of you is thinking about in
the Mekong. I know that you must still be writing
things you wouldn't even have the right to think
otherwise. You had me read things that I didn't have
the right to imagine otherwise. But I had already
done that, read in you, in your bones, remember …

I can see you running in Abidjan, you took me by
the hand. You ran faster than me along the shore of
the lagoon. Guests of Professor Déjanire, Field
Marshall Déjanire. Ah, those were good times, and
the Field Marshall, he was really something! When
we went for a walk in the evening, in the middle of
the heat wave, along the banks of the Baraboué, the
people from the Ivory Coast would watch us go by
and stop to murmur: "Shhh! It's the field marshalls!"
It's true, the Field Marshall was known throughout
the country, from the Ebrié Lagoon to Tougoukouli!

—Unèm inèseralèm, Ayehotatèm?
—Jemèb Negé.
—Menohalebet jemèb Negé.

A starlit September evening, we had taken leave of
the Field Marshall and his wife on the beach …
actually, she was his concubine … I can still see her
… And hear her … "Ah, you know, geology and
me! …" The night was so bright, we had no trouble
showing them our itinerary on the map spread out
on the sand.

Shhh … it's the … field marshalls …

You kept saying: "Listen to the sound of the lagoon …
lagoons speak all languages …" But everything was
silent. You were looking for the words, as if words
could have been among the many things one can find
in water. But water doesn't speak. The noise of water
submerges other noises, it takes on the sense of other
noises, they merge, it's not the same life, or it's a single,
great life that's drowning. A single, great confusion. It's
not the same letters, water erases the ink, people will
think it was a single, long letter, not meant for me who
will find it, but always for others …

Today I understand why you liked looking at your
face in the water of the lagoon. Part of you was
already there, that's why … Part of you was already
there, drowned, forever drowned, yet always
surviving a bit—but someone who wants to survive
is someone who has already begun to die—and
holding on to the rest of you, in the daylight, in the
streets of Abidjan, in the capital, you the scientist
whose name and face were known from Ebrié
Lagoon to Tougoukouli …

And me, who had known you for ever …

And you, who kept saying to me in Ethiopian—and
the Field Marshall's concubine (but we weren't
supposed to know and we called her his wife)
corrected your accent—you kept saying: "When I
return, I'm going to marry Carla who doesn't want to
die. Carla who confuses cities and rivers."

When you read these lines …

Water erased the other passages.

By the time you have read these lines …

Crying.

"Hélam inélaman iénen jameb
menhjiameb hiélénémaneb?"

What did they do with the rest? Where are the other
pages of this letter? Where are the pages that belong
to me? Illegible fragments in the Mekong? They
should have gone into the Mekong like him and
retrieved those pages. Where are the geologists? I
have to talk to them, where are they?

What did they write in their reports? What did they
say about these fragments of a farewell letter, did
they give the impression they knew what it said
without having read it?

A letter with so many words missing is a letter which
doesn't exist. They made sure this letter would never
exist. They took the other pages. They should be
searched, they lied, they didn't throw it into the river,
this letter exists, they lied, what is missing exists!
Search them. Get a search warrant. Go into their
homes. They must have divided up the sentences
related to them, so we have to get our hands on each
one of those excerpts, I want to read everything my
husband wrote. My husband, Anthony van Saikin,
had important things to say. He went off to that
god-forsaken part of the world to write them,
because those things were too far inside him. But you
couldn't have hidden these pages as far away as he
went to write them.

Where are the geologists? What did they do with
those pages? Where is the report on the expedition?

Where are you?

I want to know the exact place. What time is it there? ... What is the weather like? Tell me the exact time in Asia ... Tell me the time, forever ...

III

The Amur

XU SOJEN

I cried when I saw the Mekong again. I had only
cried one other time, eight years ago, when I had to
leave Cambodia. The time it took to cross the border
and reach the camp east of Bangkok. Then the flight
that took twenty-five hours. A bit longer than a day
and a night. The bitter memory is still with me. And
I didn't know that I one day would see my country
again.

The head of the Department is a cold man. Yet,
strangely enough, he had thought of announcing the
news to me the way David Lenowski would have
announced it himself. He gave me all the files, he
explained the trip, then he said: "They'll be waiting
for you on Wednesday in Phnom-Penh." It was
Monday. I got my visa and took a plane to London
that same evening. The following afternoon, I flew
on to Pakistan. And on the morning of the third day,
another plane left me off in Phnom-Penh. I had to
walk for another three hours ... In all, the trip had
taken forty-one hours, which is not so long to reach
a place that no longer exists. And I cried when I saw
the Mekong again.

—Soksai lae!
—Soksai bai gvie'tse?
—Mai kiengkai tseus.

David Lenowski was waiting for me in Phnom-Penh.
We travelled downstream. I hadn't realized the
installation had been set up in the South. I was even
quite surprised. The river was too wide below

Prak-Kèk, where they had assembled the meccano structure. The terrain was muddy, and what's more, they had chosen a location too far from the shore, but also too far from the rice paddies to get help in the case of an emergency. I shared these thoughts with Jason Cassilly. He explained that the choice had been made based on the difficulties they had encountered in the Sudan.

From afar, the installation looked like a toy. I was stupefied: the unit was hardly any higher than this. Such a small apparatus produced drinking water for continents. We were in the middle of a desert of mist and swamps. We kept sinking into the mud. It had been raining since their arrival. With considerable difficulty, we finally reached the actual campsite. And even then, it was much smaller than I had been led to believe. It's true that all the travelling made transporting gigantic pieces of equipment impossible.

They took me over to his body.

I don't know. I don't think that "reaction" or "react" is the right word. From what I know of your language, one would say "conceive." Understand that I already knew it, to a certain extent. Minus all the horror.

The strangest thing is that I recognized him. I didn't have to look at each member of the expedition in order to know which one of them was there in front of me, sitting in the silt, leaning against one of the structure's pylons. It was him, despite his beauty that had disappeared, despite his bones that one could see ... here.

—Ae vien drei'r jien?
—Tsiej ab g'hie tsian ki'k.
—Tsiao tse n'bui ai' whui …

There he was, serene, watching the end of everything. His arms open, his palms turned toward the water, he was on the other side of eternity waiting for everything to begin again.

Directly in front of him, the Mekong merged with the rains. There was none of the usual movement of those showers that hammer their way into the surface. All the water in that landscape was immobile, suspended, and you had to listen carefully to hear its song without a melody.

They should have wired Minneapolis. They would have had to walk upstream, towards the rice paddies. But it seems that no one, for some inexplicable reason, had thought of declaring an emergency. In their fear, they heard the sound of the rain as something threatening. Rain, which constitutes all things, is like a silence one can describe. It is there in the object of silence that we must look for all the words we would like to say in that part of the body where everything is obscure, where everything merges, where cries are harboured.

—Who killed him?
—He wanted to die so badly.
—Who killed him?
—We helped him die.
—Are you the one who killed him?
—No, it wasn't me.

91

On the tenth day of its decomposition, Toni van Saikin's body was in such a state that the rain, although it was very fine, struck his skull like seconds, and the drops carved crevices down his cheeks. It was those grey streaks that finally made him unrecognizable, and we decided we should close his eyes. We took a few steps toward him, then we had to retreat because of an unbearable smell that came from his skin. But we had gone just far enough to realize that he no longer had any eyelids.

I saw that he had experienced an orgasm at the very end. His penis was still erect. He had died like hanged men die, and that says a lot about the rebellion of this man who had gone looking for the idea of immediate resurrection there in its last refuge. Even in the most total darkness, the soul knows no hesitation.

The following day the rain increased. It's a shame. If only the rain had remained as it was, we could have witnessed the total metamorphosis. I knew that his soul was still a prisoner of his corpse, it could not tear itself away from Toni van Saikin as long as he continued to stare at us with his eyes which seemed to want to be last to die. His soul was huddling there in his gaze, determined to stay as long as possible in this body still caught up in dying. From its vantage point, that soul must have been looking at the members, those legs stretched out, half buried in the mud and in their own residue, with the skin that, as it detached itself from the bones, trickled in rivulets till it reached the river and the sea. One could see it being gently deported toward the mouth of a river that appeared like a gash between two grey slopes blending into the horizon at the Viet Nam border. Jason Cassilly, Lloyd Macurdy and Ralph Peterson went back to the camp. David Lenowski and I stayed to look at Toni van Saikin one last time.

In the hue of the rains, it looked like the very first moments of the universe. Those moments passed one by one, on that anarchistic head, that gaping head, open but soon to be extinguished, that brain invaded by vacuity and suspicion.

Impossible to know where one comes from. Impossible to know where one goes. Toni van Saikin's brain was watching the diffuse and chaotic infinity of the sea, there since before the beginning of the time. The engineer's brain was watching the diffuse and chaotic infinity of the sea, there since before the genesis of man and his brain.

He didn't exist, he pre-existed, he didn't pre-exist, he existed, it all comes down to the same thing when you're looking at infinity.

For a moment, David and I had the same startled jolt. One would have sworn that the dead man was about to say something and we were frightened. True, his jaw had moved. Had it been up to me, I would have waited for a long time. Perhaps he wanted to ask us a favour, or maybe he wanted to reveal some fact he felt it was important for us to know, who knows? But already, because of that movement, his face had begun to look like a skull, and, strangely enough, in no time at all, I'd say within seconds, Toni van Saikin became like all the others. His soul was already far away, over the China Sea.

David and I went back to the camp. I was exhausted. The structure was badly damaged. The roof leaked. I went up to the second storey where Toni van Saikin stored his things. I took his place and I found the pages of a letter that he had been writing since his arrival in Cambodia. I read what was legible. Water had erased several passages. Toni van Saikin had clear and deliberate handwriting. Those pages read like a book. I read the letter several times, following the order of the fragments.

Before falling into the sleep of the long night of hope, I thought of Huan Chou, the god of lightning who died piercing his own body, and whose wound foreshadowed the place where the world, as we know it, was to be born.

In the light of the fragments of this farewell letter, I still can't say why Toni van Saikin wanted to live so badly. Few men display so much credulity and tenaciousness in order to escape death and avoid the inevitable. They only succeed, however, in irritating destiny. No, I can't say why Toni van Saikin was so determined to live when it was so obvious he was going to die, but I think that he was writing this farewell letter to himself, for the day when he might return to this god-forsaken part of the world, far from all landmarks, on the banks of this river, for having written these lines ...

For the day when he might return to this god-forsaken part of the world, far from all landmarks, on the banks of this river, for having written these lines …

Mr. Chairman, Gentlemen, Madam, I thank you for your attention.

THE END